WAY

Daniel Boone

History Maker Bios

Candice Ransom

LERNER PUBLICATIONS COMPANY • MINNEAPOLIS

To Frank, my adventurous Pennsylvanian

Illustrations by Tim Parlin

Text copyright © 2005 by Candice Ransom
Illustrations copyright © 2005 by Lerner Publishing Group, Inc.

Lerner Publications Company
A division of Lerner Publishing Group, Inc.
241 First Avenue North
Minneapolis, MN 55401 U.S.A.

Website address: www.lernerbooks.com

Library of Congress Cataloging-in-Publication Data

Ransom, Candice F., 1952–
    Daniel Boone / by Candice Ransom.
      p.   cm. — (History maker bios)
    Includes bibliographical references and index.
    ISBN-13: 978–0–8225–2941–5 (lib. bdg. : alk. paper)
    ISBN-10: 0–8225–2941–6 (lib. bdg. : alk. paper)
    1. Boone, Daniel, 1734–1820—Juvenile literature. 2. Pioneers—Kentucky—Biography—Juvenile literature. 3. Explorers—Kentucky—Biography—Juvenile literature. 4. Frontier and pioneer life—Kentucky—Juvenile literature. 5. Kentucky—Biography—Juvenile literature. 6. Kentucky—Discovery and exploration—Juvenile literature. I. Title. II. Series.
F454.B66R36 2005
976.9'02'092—dc22
                                               2004028787

Manufactured in the United States of America
2 3 4 5 6 7 – JR – 12 11 10 09 08 07

TABLE OF CONTENTS

INTRODUCTION

Daniel Boone was a backwoodsman in the 1700s. He spent his whole life exploring and hunting in the wilderness.

Daniel also blazed the way west from Virginia to the green hills of Kentucky. White pioneers wanted to settle and farm this rich land. But they needed a road that crossed the rugged Appalachian Mountains. Daniel Boone built that road and made it big enough for wagons. He risked his life to lead settlers to Kentucky.

People told stories about the bears Daniel Boone killed and the Native Americans he battled. They called him a hero. But Daniel did not believe he was a hero. He wanted to live free, away from crowded towns. And he wanted to help others share the same freedom.

This is his story.

1 QUAKER BOY

On November 2, 1734, the sixth child of Sarah and Squire Boone was born in their farmhouse. They named him Daniel. Daniel's family lived in Exeter in the British colony of Pennsylvania.

The colony had been started by people who practiced the Quaker religion. The Boones were also Quakers. They believed in living simply and peacefully.

The Boones grew corn, tobacco, and vegetables on their farm. But Daniel didn't like farming. He didn't like staying put either. He would rather wander in the woods.

In Quaker meetings like this one, Daniel's mother held his hand. If she let go, he wiggled away to escape to the woods.

In the forest, Daniel loved to study the tracks of bears, mountain lions, wolves, and deer. He learned the way of the woods from older brothers and other hunters. They taught him which plants cured fever and snakebite. They showed him how to predict the weather by looking at the sky.

Daniel spent many happy hours studying the plants and animals near his home.

Native American boys from the nearby Delaware community were also Daniel's teachers. Many settlers hated Native Americans. Some of these settlers were eager to fight. Not Daniel. He believed in Quaker teachings that all people should be treated kindly. He preferred friendship to fighting.

NATIVE AMERICANS IN PENNSYLVANIA

Native Americans lived on the land that became Pennsylvania long before it was a British colony. At first, the Delaware (also called the Lenape), Shawnee, and Iroquois shared their land with the white colonists in peace. But around Daniel's time, Pennsylvania's leaders tricked the Native Americans into giving up much of their land. Many Native Americans began to see the settlers as their enemies. And many settlers began to fear and hate their Native American neighbors.

Fur traders did business with pioneers as well as Native Americans. Fur traders shipped the animal skins to Europe.

Daniel got his first hunting rifle when he was twelve or thirteen. He was happy to help his family by hunting animals or game, such as wild turkeys and deer.

Game wasn't used only for food. Deerskin was as good as money. Fur traders bought the deerskins. The skins were used for clothing, shoes, and other items.

Soon after Daniel started hunting, he killed his first mountain lion. He quickly became a better hunter than his older brothers.

Daniel began to dress like a hunter in a plain shirt and pants. Leggings protected his lower legs. Daniel walked silently in traditional Native American shoes called moccasins. He wore his dark hair in a braid topped with a broad-brimmed hat.

In the spring of 1750, Daniel's father decided to move from Pennsylvania. He had heard that good land could be found in North Carolina.

Like this hunter, Daniel wore comfortable clothing and often carried a rifle.

The Boone family and Daniel's best friend, Henry Miller, set out in covered wagons. North Carolina was five hundred miles south. Their journey would be a long one.

Fifteen-year-old Daniel helped lead the way. He walked in front with his rifle, ready to shoot game or dangerous animals. For Daniel, life on the trail was a dream come true. He guided his family by day and slept under the stars at night.

Later that spring, the Boones stopped for a while in Virginia. They pitched camp in the Shenandoah Valley.

Daniel's family traveled south in a Conestoga wagon.

Daniel and Henry decided to go on their first "long hunt." Native Americans hunted in this way, leaving their villages for weeks or months. They would bring home game to eat and valuable fur to sell.

Daniel and Henry disappeared into the mountains for months. They hunted many animals and sold the fur.

Henry Miller grew tired of hunting and wandering through the woods. When he and Daniel returned to the Boone family, Henry decided to settle down in Virginia. Not Daniel. For him, life in the wilderness was the greatest adventure.

2 LONG HUNTER

Daniel's life on the trail ended when his family reached North Carolina. Squire Boone bought land in the Yadkin River Valley. Every day, Daniel helped clear his father's land so they could build a house and plow a garden. But Daniel was as restless as ever. He would rather hunt in the woods than cut down trees.

At twenty, Daniel wasn't a tall man. But his chest and shoulders were powerful. He had sharp, blue gray eyes and an easy manner.

War broke out between the British and the French in North America. Both countries wanted to claim some of the same land for themselves. France convinced certain Native Americans to fight on their side. This war became known as the French and Indian War (1754–1783).

The French and some Native Americans fought against the British in the French and Indian War.

Daniel wanted to protect his neighbors from the fighting. He joined the army of British general Edward Braddock. There he served as a wagon driver and became friends with another driver named John Findley. Findley told Daniel stories about Kentucky. He had followed streams and Indian trails to this special land west of the Appalachian Mountains.

Findley said that the bluegrass hills in Kentucky were thick with game. Hunters practically tripped over deer! Daniel promised himself that one day he would see this wonderful land.

Daniel was eager to get past the Appalachian Mountains to Kentucky.

Women like Daniel's wife, Rebecca, kept the household going when their husbands went away on long hunts.

After he left the army, Daniel fell in love with a neighbor back in North Carolina. He married Rebecca Bryan in August 1756. Soon their first son, James, was born. Daniel still didn't like farming, but he had a family to support. It was finally time to settle down.

In 1759, Daniel took over his father's farm. But his restless spirit longed for freedom. He continued to go on long hunts. He could earn a living by selling the fur from the animals he caught.

Daniel was known to be an excellent hunter. One story tells that he killed a bear.

Daniel rambled happily over the mountains. Sometimes he lay on the ground and sang at the top of his lungs. Once he left his mark on a tree. It said "D. Boone killed a bear on tree in the year 1760."

Daniel never stopped dreaming about going further west to Kentucky. On one long hunt, he and his brother Squire searched for a route to Kentucky. But a snowstorm forced them to turn around. Daniel wondered if he would ever see the land of the bluegrass hills.

One day, Daniel's friend John Findley visited Daniel in North Carolina. Findley wanted to return to Kentucky. But he believed there was a better way to get there.

Daniel was a great woodsman. Findley knew his friend could find a faster mountain route. Daniel jumped at the chance. On May 1, 1769, Daniel and a small group of men left North Carolina. Packhorses carried their supplies.

LONG HUNTING

During his long hunts, Daniel had to survive for many months in the wilderness. He learned to read the woods the way some people read a book. Daniel looked for signs such as footprints, crushed leaves, or broken twigs. These details told him if dangerous animals or valuable game were nearby. He and other long hunters sometimes left helpful signs for each other in the woods. They often carved messages on trees to give other hunters important information.

Other white men had been to Kentucky, but no one had ever made a map. There were no roads, just dense woods covering the mountains.

Daniel guided the men across rivers and over rocks to the Warriors' Path. This old Indian trail was used by both Native American and white hunters.

Near Kentucky, Daniel found the Cumberland Gap, a narrow pass through the mountains. Daniel led the men between the Cumberland Gap's steep cliffs.

Daniel led his band of pioneers west to Kentucky through the Cumberland Gap.

When Daniel finally laid eyes on Kentucky, he was filled with excitement. Buffalo, deer, and elk grazed in the bluegrass valley. So much game!

For the next six months, Daniel and his men hunted and trapped animals for their fur. One afternoon, Daniel and another hunter were surprised by a group of Shawnees. A Shawnee warrior named Captain Will led the group.

Captain Will was angry. The white men were hunting on Shawnee land. Captain Will took the Americans' supplies and fur. He warned Daniel to go home and never return.

In May 1771, Daniel rejoined his family. He had little to show for his two years away. But he longed for Kentucky. After seeing that beautiful land, he wanted to go back.

3 ROAD BUILDER

Like Daniel, other settlers wanted to go west across the Appalachians. Colonel William Russell hired Daniel Boone to lead the first organized group of settlers to Kentucky. Daniel was ready. His brother Squire was eager to leave too.

On September 25, 1773, both Boone families arrived in Virginia. There they joined Russell and his group of settlers.

The trail to Kentucky was too narrow for wagons. Packhorses carried household goods. Babies rode in baskets. Older children walked, leading cattle and hogs. The line of settlers snaked slowly over the mountains.

Soon the settlers needed more food. Daniel sent his sixteen-year-old son James and two young boys to Virginia for flour.

The path to Kentucky was too narrow for wagons, so pioneers traveled on horseback and on foot.

Daniel's son James was killed in an attack by Native Americans in 1773.

On the way back, the boys were attacked by a party of Delaware, Shawnee, and Cherokee men. These Native Americans were angry. The United States had promised them that white settlers wouldn't move to their hunting grounds west of the mountains. The angry Native Americans killed the boys.

News of the killing frightened the settlers with Daniel. They fled to Virginia. Daniel went back to the place of the attack the following spring. As he sat by his son's grave, it began to rain. He had never felt so sad in his entire life.

Daniel missed his son terribly. But he did not give up his dreams for the future. He and the other settlers were determined to make Kentucky their home.

Businessman Richard Henderson also wanted to start a settlement in Kentucky. He knew that settlers needed a better road across the mountains. It needed to be wide enough for wagons. He asked Daniel to build that road.

Daniel quickly hired thirty workers. His daughter Susannah and a slave woman would cook for the men.

Daniel was hired to build a road that would make traveling to Kentucky easier for pioneer families.

Daniel's group headed into the mountains in March 1775. The crew chopped down trees, burned brush, and hacked tall grass called cane.

At first, the road followed the Warriors' Path to the Cumberland Gap. Then Daniel realized that wagons could not cross into Kentucky using the old trail. It was too narrow. He left the Warriors' Path and guided the road crew to bison trails. Large herds traveled on the same path.

In the late 1700s, bison were plentiful in Kentucky. Daniel used bison trails as a base for his road.

The road that Daniel made cuts through the forest near the Cumberland Gap.

Daniel's crew slashed a path through deep forests, up and down hillsides. They hauled logs over creeks and dragged fallen trees out of the way. The road was muddy, steep, and rocky. Snow and freezing rain made the job harder.

Daniel went ahead to mark the trail. He also hunted game for supper. The men slept on the ground, worn out by the day's work. They gained new energy when they finally glimpsed the bluegrass hills of Kentucky.

On March 25, while the men slept, Native Americans fired into their camp. Two white men were killed. One was seriously wounded. Daniel nursed the wounded man using healing plants. But he couldn't stop some of his workers from returning home.

Daniel was determined to finish his road. He found a site for a settlement at the road's end. It was a perfect piece of land along the Kentucky River.

THE WILDERNESS ROAD

The trail Daniel blazed to Kentucky became a major path for thousands of settlers seeking a new life in the West. These pioneers called Daniel's trail the Wilderness Road. In the 1920s, the Wilderness Road became part of a modern highway known as U.S. Route 25. Then in 2002, workers removed the highway's pavement and restored Daniel's original trail to a wide dirt path. Trees have been planted along the path to match the forest of Daniel's time.

After more than a month of hard work, the men cut the last section of the road to the site Daniel had marked. As the crew made their way down the last hill, they came upon a huge herd of bison. The sight filled everyone with awe.

On April 20, businessman Richard Henderson arrived with another group of men. Log huts had already been built near two springs. Daniel and his men greeted Henderson's group by shooting guns into the sky. Thanks to Daniel and his new road, eighty settlers had made it to Kentucky.

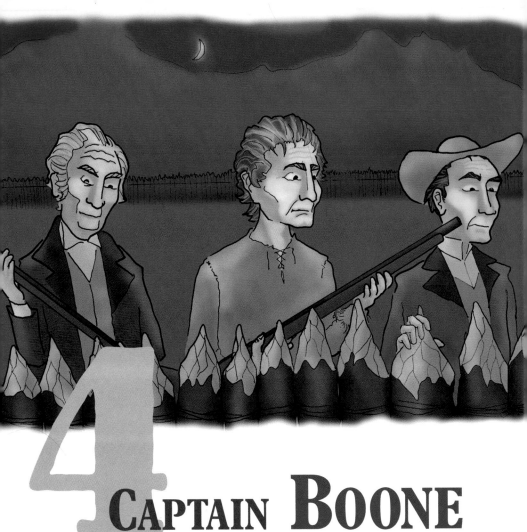

4 CAPTAIN BOONE

In early September 1775, Daniel rode into Kentucky with his wife and seven children. Daniel's men had named the Kentucky settlement Boonesborough in his honor.

Other men had also brought their families to Boonesborough. Many people lived in huts near the river. During heavy rains, the river would overflow its banks and flood their homes. The huts were dark with a few pieces of furniture on the dirt floor. The walls were hung with rifles and clothing.

Daniel wanted his family to live well. He built a sturdy cabin on higher ground. His house had wooden floors, doors, and windows with glass panes.

More settlers trickled into Kentucky. They created other settlements, but Boonesborough became one of the largest.

Boone's Fort was the first thing built in Boonesborough.

Like the other settlements, Boonesborough had its own fort. Its high log walls and heavy gate protected settlers from wild animals and attacks by Native Americans. Some Shawnees and other Native Americans wanted to drive the settlers out of Kentucky.

A few days before Christmas, a young man was shot by Shawnee fighters. Many people threw their belongings across packhorses and fled. Others left their cabins and crowded into cramped huts inside forts.

WHY PIONEERS WENT WEST

Many people and families risked their comfort and safety to move to the western frontier. The pioneers had different reasons for taking these risks. A large number of them hoped to claim cheap farming land for themselves. Others traveled west to hunt game for its valuable fur. Still others wanted to leave their old life behind for the adventure of a new life out West.

Shawnees capture
Daniel's daughter and
two of her friends.

One July
afternoon in 1776,
Daniel's fourteen-year-
old daughter Jemima went to the
river with two friends. Daniel had warned
Jemima to stay near the shore. But the girls
paddled downstream in a canoe. Suddenly,
five Native Americans grabbed their canoe
and forced them to shore.

Daniel heard the girls' screams. He ran out
of the fort, yelling for help. For two days,
Daniel and his men tracked the kidnappers.
The girls had secretly left clues for the men,
such as broken branches and shoe prints.

Daniel found the girls and took them back to Boonesborough.

At last, Daniel found the girls huddled against a tree. Daniel fired into the camp and wounded one of the Shawnee captors. The others ran away. When Daniel realized the girls were safe, he cried. News of his bravery spread through the colonies. He was becoming famous.

In August, settlers in Kentucky learned about the Revolutionary War (1775–1783). The United States was fighting for its freedom from Great Britain. Daniel knew that U.S. soldiers who guarded the settlements would leave to fight the war. Who would protect the settlers?

Daniel and twenty-two settlers decided to guard Boonesborough themselves. Daniel became captain of the Boonesborough Fort. On April 24, 1777, some Shawnees shot one of the settlers. Captain Boone and his soldiers fired back. A bullet struck Daniel's ankle, smashing the bone. He could not walk for several weeks.

A powerful leader named Chief Blackfish led the Shawnee. The chief and two hundred warriors stormed Boonesborough Fort. Daniel hobbled on a crutch, giving orders to his men.

Boonesborough settlers defend the fort against the Shawnee attack.

Daniel knew Boonesborough was in trouble. The settlers were protected inside the fort. But they were running out of water and food. If they didn't get help, they would die of thirst or starve.

News of Boonesborough's troubles reached the U.S. government. That summer, one hundred fighters came to Kentucky to defend the settlers. Another hundred friends and relatives from Daniel's old homes in North Carolina and Virginia also came to the rescue.

The settlers at Boonesborough had to wait a long time for outside help. Most of the country's soldiers were fighting against the British in the Revolutionary War.

That winter, Daniel took thirty men to lower Blue Licks Springs. These saltwater springs were forty miles from the fort. The men worked for weeks boiling water to make salt. They planned to use the salt to flavor and preserve meat, or keep it from spoiling.

One day, when Daniel was out hunting, four Shawnee men surprised him. He ran, but the warriors caught him. They took him to Chief Blackfish.

In the Shawnee village, more than a hundred Shawnee men surrounded Daniel. Blackfish told Daniel he was going to kill the settlers at the springs. Then he was going to destroy Boonesborough.

5 AMERICAN HERO

Daniel thought fast. The lives of many people depended on him. He convinced Blackfish to keep him and his men alive.

Although Daniel was a prisoner, he treated the Shawnee with respect. Blackfish soon accepted the brave and skillful white man as a member of his tribe. The Shawnee named Daniel "Big Turtle."

In June 1778, Daniel learned that Blackfish planned to attack Boonesborough. He had to escape and warn the settlers. He hopped on a horse and galloped through the woods. When the horse gave out, Daniel ran through the wilderness.

After four days, Daniel arrived at the fort. At first, people did not recognize him. They thought he was a Shawnee until he explained who he was.

Daniel learned that Rebecca had taken their children back to Yadkin. She believed he was dead. Daniel wanted to find Rebecca. But first, he had to save Boonesborough.

Daniel had been living among the Shawnee for six months when he made his escape.

Daniel led Boonesborough in its battle against the Shawnee.

On September 7, 1778, an army of four hundred Shawnee arrived at the settlement. Blackfish demanded that Daniel give up the fort. Daniel had only thirty men and twenty boys in his army. But his men voted to fight. Daniel said he would die with them.

Daniel directed his soldiers in a tough battle. After eleven days of shooting, the Shawnee gave up. Once again, people said Daniel was a hero.

That fall Daniel went to North Carolina to get his family. They returned home to Kentucky. But trouble was still brewing.

Native Americans continued to fight for their land in Kentucky. Daniel's son Israel died in a battle near Blue Licks Springs. Saddened by his son's death, Daniel needed a change. In 1783, he moved his family to another town.

One day, a schoolteacher named John Filson spoke with Daniel. He was writing a book about Kentucky. Daniel enjoyed talking about his early life in Kentucky. "The Adventures of Colonel Daniel Boone" was published in 1784 as part of Filson's book. It included exciting stories of Daniel's bravery as a hunter and trailblazer.

Stories about Daniel Boone are included in Filson's book, DISCOVERY, SETTLEMENT, AND PRESENT STATE OF KENTUCKE.

THE
ADVENTURES
OF
COLONEL DANIEL BOON,
FORMERLY A HUNTER:
Containing a NARRATIVE of the WARS of
KENTUCKY.

CURIOSITY is natural to the ſoul of man and intereſting objects have a powerful influence on our affections. Let theſe influencing powers actuate, by the permiſſion or diſpoſal of Providence, from ſelfiſh or ſocial views, yet in time the myſterious will of Heaven is unfolded, and we behold our conduct, from whatſoever motives excited, operating to anſwer the important deſigns of heaven. Thus we behold Kentucky, lately an howling wilderneſs, the habitation of ſavages and wild beaſts, become a fruitful field ; this region, ſo favourably diſtinguiſhed by nature, now become the habitation of civilization, at a period unparalleled in hiſtory, in the midſt of a raging war, and under all the diſadvantages of emigration to a country ſo remote from the inhabited

Daniel's fame spread all over the United States and even to Europe. People called Daniel an original American hero. Daniel didn't want extra attention. At the same time, Kentucky was becoming too crowded for him. Towns and farms had replaced the settlements. Game was harder to find.

In 1799, Daniel decided to move to present-day Missouri. He built a cabin overlooking the Missouri River. Happily, he went on long hunts with his sons.

AN ORDINARY MAN

Daniel always wanted to live a simple life away from large towns and crowds. Sometimes curious people tried to visit his home to meet the living legend. If Daniel saw these strangers coming, he would grab his cane and wander off into the woods. He did not think of himself as a hero. He simply loved nature. In Daniel's mind, he was just an ordinary man.

Some Shawnee also came west. Both Daniel and the Native Americans put their fighting days behind them. "Big Turtle" was glad to go hunting with the Shawnee.

Daniel found hunting tougher than it used to be. He was in his sixties. His joints were stiff from years of walking on cold, wet ground. One day, he took a chill in the woods. That was his last hunt. He spent his days telling his grandchildren stories.

On the morning of September 26, 1820, a dying Daniel said good-bye to his family. "I am going," he said. "My time has come." Those were Daniel Boone's last words. He was eighty-five years old.

So many people came to Daniel's funeral that they did not fit in the house. The service was held around back instead. Daniel, who never liked being inside houses, would have approved.

TIMELINE

In the year . . .

1746 Daniel probably received his first rifle and became a skilled hunter.

1750 he left Pennsylvania with his family. `Age 15`

1755 his family settled in North Carolina in the Yadkin River Valley.
he fought in the French and Indian War.

1756 he married Rebecca Bryan on August 14. `Age 21`

1769 he made his first trip to Kentucky.

1773 Daniel's son James was killed during an attack by Native Americans.

1775 Daniel built a trail to Kentucky with thirty men. The trail is later called the Wilderness Road.
the Revolutionary War began.

1776 he rescued his daughter Jemima from being kidnapped by the Shawnee. `Age 41`

1778 he was captured by the Shawnee and accepted as a member of the tribe.
he escaped and returned to defend Boonesborough against a Shawnee attack.

1782 his son Israel was killed an a battle near Blue Licks Springs. `Age 47`

1783 the Revolutionary War ended, and the United States was a free nation.

1784 John Filson's "The Adventures of Colonel Daniel Boone" was published as part of a larger book.

1792 Kentucky became the nation's fifteenth state. `Age 57`

1799 Daniel moved with his family to Missouri.

1820 Daniel died on September 26. `Age 85`

A HERO REMEMBERED

After Daniel died, he became more famous than ever. The stories that John Filson wrote about were retold by other writers and storytellers. The tales became more exciting and less true in each retelling. Even the clothing Daniel wore was exaggerated. People began saying that he always wore a hat made from raccoon fur. This coonskin hat showed up in paintings and plays about Daniel. But that kind of hat is something Daniel never wore.

In modern times, Daniel has remained a popular hero of the past. Towns, roads, rivers, and mountains have been named after him. His stories have been retold in movies, radio programs, comic strips, and even a television show. Many of these stories show Daniel with his coonskin cap. They tell tales that are not always true. But they all remind us of Daniel's true courage and his love of the wilderness.

FURTHER READING

NONFICTION
Aller, Susan Bivin. *Tecumseh.* Minneapolis: Lerner Publications Company, 2004. Describes the life and times of the famous Shawnee leader.

Brown, Dottie. *Kentucky.* Minneapolis: Lerner Publications Company, 2002. Includes information about the geography, history, economy, and people of this state.

Dean, Arlan. *The Wilderness Road: From the Shenandoah Valley to the Ohio River.* New York: Powerkids Press, 2003. Describes Daniel's famous trail from Virginia to Kentucky.

Erickson, Paul. *Daily Life in a Covered Wagon.* New York: Puffin Books, 1997. Describes the adventures and challenges of life for a pioneer family in the 1800s.

Maestro, Betsy. *Struggle for a Continent: The French and Indian Wars, 1689–1763.* New York: HarperCollins, 2000. Explores the way European nations fought over control of North America, the tensions that arose between Native Americans and colonists, and the French and Indian War.

Marquette, Scott. *The Revolutionary War.* Vero Beach, FL: Rourke Publishing, 2003. Presents the events leading up to and included in our nation's fight for independence from Great Britain.

FICTION
Lawlor, Laurie. *Adventure of the Wilderness Road.* New York: Aladdin Books, 2001. Eleven-year-old Elizabeth Poage and her family become pioneers when they take Daniel Boone's new road to Boonesborough, Kentucky.

WEBSITES

Daniel Boone
http://www.earlyamerica.com/lives/boone/index.html
This history website allows visitors to read some of John
Filson's original writings about Daniel Boone's life.

Daniel Boone National Forest
http://www.southernregion.fs.fed.us/boone/
The official website of the national forest in Kentucky named
after Daniel includes a link to photographs of the forest.

Driving the Wilderness Trail
http://www.danielboonetrail.com
Established by the Daniel Boone Wilderness Trail
Association, this website describes and includes links to
information about Daniel's famous path to the West.

SELECT BIBLIOGRAPHY

Bakeless, John. *Daniel Boone: Master of the Wilderness.*
New York: William Morrow & Co., 1939.

Brown, John Mason. *Daniel Boone and the Opening of the
Wilderness.* New York: Random, 1952.

Draper, Lyman C. *The Life of Daniel Boone.*
Mechanicsville, PA: Stackpole, 1998.

Faragher, John Mack. *Daniel Boone: The Life and Legend
of an American Pioneer.* New York: Holt, 1992.

Lofaro, Michael A. *Daniel Boone: An American Life.*
Lexington: University Press of Kentucky, 2003.

INDEX

Acknowledgments

The images in this book are used with permission of: © Bettmann/CORBIS, p. 4; © North Wind Picture Archives, pp. 10, 11, 12, 17, 25, 39; Library of Congress, pp. 7 (LC-USZ62-5808), 34 (LC-USZ62-1431), 45 (LC-USZ62-37338); © PhotoDisc Royalty Free by Getty Images, pp. 8, 26; © Kean Collection/Getty Images, p. 15; © Annie Griffiths Belt/CORBIS, p. 16; © Jim Zuckerman/CORBIS, p. 18; Virginia State Library and Archives, p. 20; Collection of Washington University, St. Louis, p. 23; © Mary Evans Picture Library, p. 24; © David Muench/CORBIS, p. 27; The Filson Club, p. 31; © MPI/Getty Images, pp. 33, 35; National Archives, War & Conflict Collection, p. 36; © Alan Briere/ SuperStock, p. 40; Courtesy, Archiving Early America, p.41.
Front cover: Independent Picture Service
Back cover: Courtesy, Archiving Early America